HUMANIST MANIFESTO 2000

HUMANIST MANIFESTO 2000

A CALL FOR A NEW PLANETARY HUMANISM

Drafted by PAUL KURTZ

Prometheus Books

59 John Glenn Drive
Amherst, New York 14228-2119

Published 2000 by Prometheus Books

The American Humanist Association (AHA), which holds the copyrights to *Humanist Manifesto I* as well as *Humanist Manifesto II*, has played a significant role in the development of humanist philosophy in the twentieth century, and continues to do so today. The AHA is the successor organization to the Humanist Fellowship which published *Humanist Manifesto I* in 1933, and is publisher of the *Humanist* magazine, in which *Humanist Manifesto II* appeared in 1973. *Humanist Manifesto II* was the product of an open process involving a broad base of humanist contributors.

Humanist Manifesto I and *II* (with a new preface by Paul Kurtz) were published by Prometheus Books in 1973. This edition was copyrighted by Prometheus Books.

A Secular Humanist Declaration was published in *Free Inquiry* in 1980 and is copyrighted by the Council for Secular Humanism. A Prometheus Books edition was published in 1980.

A Declaration of Global Interdependence was published in *Free Inquiry* in 1988 and was endorsed by the International Academy of Humanism and the International Humanist and Ethical Union. It is copyrighted by the Council for Secular Humanism.

Humanist Manifesto II, A Secular Humanist Declaration, and *A Declaration of Global Interdependence* were drafted by Paul Kurtz.

Inquiries should be addressed to Prometheus Books, 59 John Glenn Drive, Amherst, New York 14228-2119 VOICE: 716-691-0133, ext. 210. FAX: 716-691-0137.

WWW.PROMETHEUSBOOKS.COM

17 16   15 14

Library of Congress Cataloging-in-Publication Data

Humanist manifesto 2000 : a call for a new planetary humanism / drafted by Paul Kurtz.
     p.   cm.
ISBN 13: 978-1-57392-783-3
ISBN 10: 1-57392-783-X

1. Humanism. I. Kurtz, Paul, 1925–   . II. Title.

99-050116
CIP

Printed in the United States of America on acid-free paper

TABLE OF CONTENTS

HUMANIST MANIFESTO 2000
A Call for a New Planetary Humanism

I
PREAMBLE

Humanism is an ethical, scientific, and philosophical outlook that has changed the world. Its heritage traces back to the philosophers and poets of ancient Greece and Rome, Confucian China, and the Carvaka movement in classical India. Humanist artists, writers, scientists, and thinkers have been shaping the modern era for over half a millennium. Indeed, humanism and modernism have often seemed synonymous; for humanist ideas and values express a renewed confidence in the power of human beings to solve their own problems and conquer uncharted frontiers.

Modern humanism came to fruition during the Renaissance. It led to the development of modern science. During the Enlightenment it germinated new ideals of social justice and inspired the democratic revolutions of our time. Humanism has helped frame a new ethical outlook emphasizing the values of freedom and happiness and the virtues of universal human rights.

The signers of this *Manifesto* believe that humanism has

much to offer humanity as we face the problems of the twenty-first century and the new millennium beyond. Many of the old ideas and traditions that humankind has inherited are no longer relevant to current realities and future opportunities. We need fresh thinking if we are to cope with the global society that is now emerging, and fresh thinking is the hallmark of humanism. Therefore we present *Humanist Manifesto 2000: A Call for a New Planetary Humanism.*

The following recommendations are offered in modesty but with the conviction that they can contribute to a dialogue among the different cultural, political, economic, and religious viewpoints in the world. Although we who endorse this document share common principles and values, we are prepared to modify our views in the light of new knowledge, altered circumstances, and unforeseen problems that may arise. It is not possible to create a permanent Manifesto, but it is useful and wise to devise a working document, open to revision.

Prologue to the Present

Four major *Humanist Manifestos* and *Declarations* have already been issued in the twentieth century: *Humanist Manifesto I, Humanist Manifesto II, A Secular Humanist Declaration,* and *A Declaration of Interdependence.*

Humanist Manifesto I appeared in 1933 at the height of the world depression. Endorsed by thirty-four American humanists (including philosopher John Dewey), it reflected the concerns of that time, recommending first a form of nontheistic religious humanism as an alternative to the religions of the age, and, second, national economic and social planning. *Humanist Manifesto II* was released in 1973 to deal with the issues that had emerged on the world scene since then: the rise of fascism and its defeat in the Second World War, the growth in influence and power of Marxism-Leninism and Maoism, the Cold War, the postwar economic recovery of Europe and America, the decolonialization of large sectors of the world, the creation of the United Nations, the sexual revolution, the growth of the women's movement, the demand of minorities for equal rights, and the emergence of student power on the campuses.

That *Manifesto* stimulated widespread debate. It was signed by many leaders of thought and action throughout the world: Andreï Sakharov, noted Soviet dissident; Julian Huxley, former President of UNESCO; Sidney Hook; Betty Friedan; Gunnar Myrdal; Jacques Monod; Francis Crick; Margaret Knight; Allan Guttmacher; James Farmer; Ritchie Calder; and A. Philip Randolph, among others. It defended human rights on a global scale, arguing for the right to travel beyond national frontiers at a time when people behind the Iron Curtain were prohibited from doing so. Many Marxist humanists in Eastern Europe had attacked totalitarian statism and welcomed a defense of democracy and human rights.

Humanist Manifesto II no longer defended a planned economy, but left the question open to alternative economic systems. Thus, it was endorsed by both liberals and economic libertarians, who defended a free market, as well as by social democrats and democratic socialists, who believed that the government should have a substantial role to play in a welfare society. It sought to democratize economic systems and test them by whether or not they increased economic well-being for all individuals and groups.

Humanist Manifesto II was written when a new moral revolution seemed upon us: it defended the right to birth control, abortion, divorce, sexual freedom between consenting adults, and euthanasia. It sought to protect the rights of minorities, women, the elderly, abused children, and the disadvantaged. It advocated tolerance of alternative lifestyles and the peaceful negotiation of differences, and it deplored racial, religious, and class antagonisms. It called for an end to terror and hatred. It was written in the wake of Vatican II, which had attempted to liberalize Roman Catholicism. *Humanist Manifesto II* left room for both naturalistic humanism and liberal religious humanism. The *Manifesto* was optimistic about the prospects for humankind. It pointed to the benefits of science and technology for human good. It predicted that the twenty-first century could become the humanist century.

A Secular Humanist Declaration was issued in 1980 because humanism, and especially *Humanist Manifesto II*, had come under heavy attack, particularly from fundamentalist religious and right-wing political forces in the United States. Many of these critics maintained that secular humanism was a *religion.* The teaching of secular humanism in the schools, they claimed, violated the principle of the separation of church and state and established a new religion. The *Declaration* responded that secular humanism expressed a set of moral values and a nontheistic philosophical and scientific viewpoint that could not be equated with religious faith. The teaching of the secular humanist outlook in no way was a violation of the separation principle. It defended the democratic idea that the secular state should be neutral, neither for nor against religion. In 1988, the International Academy of Humanism offered still a fourth document, *A Declaration of Interdependence*, calling for a new global ethics and the building of a world community, which were increasingly necessary in view of the global institutions that were rapidly evolving.

Why Planetary Humanism?

While most of the provisions of these earlier *Manifestos* and *Declarations* are still viable, it is apparent that as the world enters a new millennium a new *Manifesto* is necessary. Since the earlier *Manifestos*, while much progress has been made, new circumstances have emerged to challenge us: Totalitarian communism has collapsed in the Soviet Union and Eastern Europe and the two-power Cold War blocs have largely dissipated. New sectors of the globe have attempted to become more democratic, though many countries still lack effective democratic institutions. Moreover, the world economy has become even more globalized. International conglomerates have merged and become transnational and, in a sense, more powerful than many nations in the world. Russia, China, and other countries have sought to enter the world market. No one country is able to master its economic destiny independent of world trade and commerce. These fundamental changes have occurred largely because of the accelerated growth of science and technology, and especially the information revolution, which has led to a worldwide economic and cultural communications network. Arguably the changes wrought in the world since *Humanist Manifesto II* are as great or greater than those of the Industrial Revolution two centuries ago, or the invention by Gutenberg of moveable type and the printing press. The repercussions to our global existence will continue to be enormous.

Yet, as the world becomes a global family, ethnic-religious rivalries have sought to divide territories into contending factions. Fundamentalist religions have rekindled, contesting the principles of humanism and secularism and demanding a return to the religiosity of a premodern era. So-called New Age paranormal beliefs likewise have emerged, abetted by the mass media touting a spiritual/paranormal view of reality. The media have been globalized. TV, films, radio, and book and magazine publishers are dominated by media conglomerates, concerned almost solely with advertising and selling products to the world market. In addition, postmodernism has appeared in many universities, questioning the basic premises of modernity and humanism, attacking science and technology, and questioning humanist ideals and values. Many current visions of the future are pessimistic, even apocalyptic. But we object for we believe that it is possible to create a better world. The realities of the global society are such that only a new Planetary Humanism can provide meaningful directions for the future.

II
PROSPECTS FOR A BETTER FUTURE

For the first time in human history we possess the means–provided by science and technology–to ameliorate the human condition, advance happiness and freedom, and enhance human life for *all* people on the planet. Many people who talk about the new millennium are fearful about what will ensue. Many make doomsday forecasts about coming calamities–whether religious or secular. Pessimists point to the brutal wars of the twentieth century and warn that new forms of terrorism and unrest may engulf humanity in the coming century.

We think that a more positive and realistic appraisal of the human prospect in the twenty-first century is in order. We wish to point out that in spite of political, military, and social unrest, the twentieth century has witnessed a great number of beneficent achievements. However disappointing to naysayers, prosperity, peace, better health, and rising standards of living are a reality–and likely to continue. These great technological, scientific, and social achievements have often been overlooked. Although they apply largely to the developed world, their benefits are now being felt virtually everywhere. We need to list some of them:

- Scientific medicine has improved health enormously. It has reduced pain and suffering, and it has increased longevity. The discovery of antibiotics and the development of vaccines, modern techniques of surgery, anesthesia, pharmacology, and biogenetic engineering have all contributed to these advances in health care.

• Farsighted public health measures and improved water supplies and sewage disposal have greatly reduced the incidence of infectious disease. Therapeutic remedies, widely applied, have dramatically reduced child mortality.

• The Green Revolution has transformed food production and increased crop yields, reduced hunger, and raised the levels of nutrition for large portions of the globe.

• Modern methods of mass production have increased productivity, liberated workers from many forms of physical drudgery, and made possible the benefits and luxuries of consumer goods and services.

• New modes of transportation have reduced distances and transformed societies. The automobile and airplane have enabled people to traverse continents and overcome geographical isolation. Astronautical research has opened the human species to the exciting adventure of space exploration.

• Technological discoveries have vastly accelerated new modes of communication on a worldwide basis. In addition to the benefits of telephone, fax, radio, TV, and satellite transmission, computer technology has radically transformed all aspects of socioeconomic life. No office or home in the developed world is untouched by the information revolution. The Internet and the World Wide Web have made possible instant communication almost everywhere on the globe.

- Scientific research has expanded our knowledge of the universe and the place of the human species within it. Human inquiry is now able to advance and to have its findings confirmed by science and reason, while the metaphysical and theological speculations of the past have made little or no progress. The discoveries of astronomy, physics, relativity theory, and quantum mechanics have increased our understanding of the universe—from the scale of microparticles to that of galaxies. Biology and genetics have contributed to our knowledge of the biosphere. Darwin's nineteenth-century theory of natural selection has enabled us to understand how life evolved. The discoveries of DNA and molecular biology continue to reveal the mechanisms of evolution and of life itself. The behavioral and social sciences have deepened our knowledge of social and political institutions, the economy, and culture.

Many positive social and political developments have also occurred in the twentieth century and these bode well for the future:

- The colonial empires of the nineteenth century have all but disappeared.

Humanist Manifesto 2000

- The threat of totalitarianism has abated.

- *The Universal Declaration of Human Rights* is now accepted by most nations of the world (in word if not in deed).

- The ideals of democracy, freedom, and the open society have spread widely to Eastern Europe, Latin America, Asia, and Africa.

- Women in many countries now enjoy personal autonomy and legal and social rights, and have taken their place in many areas of human enterprise.

- As national economies have become globalized, economic prosperity has been carried from Europe and North America to other parts of the world. Free markets and entrepreneurial methods have opened underdeveloped regions to capital investment and development.

- The problem of population growth has been resolved in the affluent countries of Europe and North America. In many areas the population grows not because of the birth rate but because of the decline of the death rate and the increase of longevity—a positive development.

- Increased education, literacy, and cultural enrichment are now available to more and more children in the world—though there is still much more that needs to be done.

In spite of these breakthroughs, we need squarely to confront the severe economic, social, and political problems the world still faces. The prophets of doom are pessimistic; the Jeremiahs predict misfortune and calamity. We respond that, if our problems are to be solved, it will be only by marshaling reason, science, and human endeavor.

- Large sectors of the world population still do not enjoy the fruits of affluence; they continue to languish in poverty, hunger, and disease, particularly in the developing world, in Asia, Africa, and Central and South America. Millions of children and adults live at a subsistence level with poor nutrition, sanitation, and health. This applies to many people in the so-called affluent societies as well.

- Population continues to grow in many parts of the world at the annual rate of 3 percent. In 1900 the world had an estimated 1.7 billion people. By the year 2000 it will exceed 6 billion. If present demographic trends continue, another 3 billion people will be added in the next half century.

- If population continues to grow as projected, it will lead to a drastic decrease in the available tillable grain lands, which may by 2050 shrink to one-quarter of an acre per person in many countries (notably in India, Pakistan, Ethiopia, Nigeria, and Iran). Freshwater supplies for irrigation are already overtaxed, reducing crop yields;

many of the world's rivers are beginning to run dry (including the Nile, the Colorado River, and the Yellow River in China).

• As human populations have expanded and industrial development has accelerated, rain forests and timberlands have been devastated. An estimated 2 percent of the earth's forests are disappearing annually. This toll will continue unless preventive measures are undertaken.

• Global warming is probably on the increase, in part as a consequence of deforestation in poor countries and atmospheric carbon-dioxide emissions, especially in the affluent nations, which continue to waste natural resources. The average person in the United States and other Western countries consumes and pollutes an estimated forty to sixty times as much as the average person in the developing world. Wasteful consumption is often encouraged by growth-oriented companies, with too little concern for the ecological fallout.

• The populations of other species have steadily declined, and many forms of plant and animal life are becoming extinct—perhaps the greatest extinction since the disappearance of the dinosaurs sixty-five million years ago.

• Many governments of the world are facing severe economic problems as cities overflow with immigrants from the countryside; vast numbers of them are unemployed and barely able to subsist.

- Unemployment remains a serious problem in many of the affluent countries of Europe as well, which are failing to absorb young workers, retool technology, retrain employees, or find them jobs.

- Wide-ranging agreements for tackling many of the international social and environmental problems facing humanity were achieved in an important series of international conferences, but governments have failed to live up to the commitments made; few of the richer countries give any priority to helping the poor majority, or even to helping the alienated and dispossessed in their own societies.

- Democracy remains weak or nonexistent in many countries. Too often the free press is muzzled and elections are thwarted.

- Failure to accord equal rights to women is still widespread in most of the countries of the world.

- Many of the former colonial areas have fallen into economic decline.

- Diseases once thought to be conquered, such as tuberculosis and malaria, are on the increase, while HIV/AIDS is running unchecked in large parts of the developing world.

- Though the world is no longer divided into two superpowers, humankind still has the power to destroy itself.

Fanatical terrorists, rogue states, or even the major powers can inadvertently trigger apocalyptic events by unleashing weapons of mass destruction.

- The belief in some quarters that the free market will cure all social problems remains a *faith*. How to balance the demands of the free market with the need for equitable social programs to assist the disadvantaged and impoverished remains an unresolved issue in many countries of the world.

We grant that these are serious problems, and we need to take adequate measures to resolve them. We believe that only with the use of critical intelligence and cooperative efforts can they be overcome. Humankind has faced challenges in the past and has managed to persevere, even to triumph. The problems looming on the horizon are perhaps no greater than those our forebears faced.

There are still other dangerous tendencies in the world that are insufficiently recognized. We are especially concerned about antiscientific, antimodern trends, including the emergence of shrill fundamentalist voices and the persistence of bigotry and intolerance, whether religious, political, or tribal in origin. These are the same forces in many parts of the world that oppose efforts to resolve social problems or to ameliorate the human condition:

- The persistence of traditional spiritual attitudes often encourages unrealistic, escapist, otherwordly approaches to social problems, inculcates a disrespect for science, and all too often defends archaic social institutions.

- Many religious and political groups oppose contraception or the funding of programs designed to reduce fertility and to stabilize population growth. As a result, economic development and the reduction of poverty are hampered.

- Many of these forces also oppose the liberation of women and wish to keep them subservient to men.

- The world increasingly has witnessed bitter ethnic conflicts and intensified tribal rivalries. The religious dimensions to these conflicts remain largely unreported: in Yugoslavia among Serbian Orthodox Christians, Croatian Roman Catholics, and Muslims (in Bosnia and Kosovo); in Israel and Palestine between Orthodox Jews and Muslims; in Northern Ireland between Protestants and Catholics; in Sri Lanka between Tamil Hindus and Sinhalese Buddhists; in the Punjab and Kashmir among Hindus, Muslims, and Sikhs; in East Timor between Christians and Muslims.

- The world is rightly concerned by the growth of terrorism and genocide, again too frequently inflamed by ethnic nationalists or religious chauvinists.

- Multiculturalism advocates the toleration of diverse ethnic and cultural traditions and a recognition of their right to exist. But we have also seen a fracturing of society and the demand for separation and isolation, ironically at a time when Nazi racist doctrines and apartheid in South Africa have been thoroughly repudiated. Intolerance has generated ethnic cleansing and other virulent manifestations of racial hatred.

• There has emerged in many Western countries a so-called postmodernist ideology that denies the objectivity of science, deplores the use of modern technology, and attacks human rights and democracy. Some forms of postmodernism counsel defeatism: at best, they offer no program for resolving the world's problems; at worst, they deny that solutions are either possible or achievable. The effects of this philosophical-literary movement are counterproductive, even nihilistic. We think it profoundly mistaken because science does offer reasonably objective standards for judging its truth claims. Indeed, science has become a universal language, speaking to all men and women no matter what their cultural backgrounds.

We believe that it is necessary to present an alternative vision of tomorrow. National governments and corporate leaders must abandon short-term policies and support forward-looking planning. All too often these leaders ignore the best advice of scientists and humanists and base their policies on the upcoming election or on the next quarterly earnings report. National governments must not only be concerned with immediate economic or political considerations, but pay attention to the needs of the entire planet and a sustainable future for humankind.

Planetary Humanism seeks to recommend long-range attainable goals. This is a principal distinction between humanism and premodern, religiously based moralities. Humanism formulates courageous new images of the future and generates confidence in the ability of the human species to solve its problems by rational means and a positive outlook.

The eighteenth-century Enlightenment, which has inspired this *Manifesto*, was no doubt limited by the times in which it appeared. Its view of Reason as an absolute rather than as a tentative and fallible instrument of human purpose was overdrawn. Nevertheless, its conviction that science, reason, democracy, education, and humanist values could enhance human progress still has great appeal to us today. The Planetary Humanism that this *Manifesto* presents is *post*-postmodernist in its outlook. It draws on the best values of modernity, yet it seeks to transcend the negativity of postmodernism and it looks forward to the information age now dawning and all that this portends for the future of humankind.

III
SCIENTIFIC NATURALISM

The unique message of humanism on the current world scene is its commitment to scientific naturalism. Most worldviews accepted today are spiritual, mystical, or theological in character. They have their origins in the ancient preurban, nomadic, and agricultural societies of the past, not in the modern industrial or postindustrial global information culture that is emerging. Scientific naturalism enables human beings to construct a coherent worldview disentangled from metaphysics or theology and based on the sciences.

- First, *scientific naturalism is committed to a set of methodological prescriptions.* For methodological naturalism, all hypotheses and theories must be tested experimentally by reference to natural causes and events. It is inadmissible to introduce occult causes or transcendental explanations. The methods of science are not infallible, they do not present us with unchanging, absolute truths; yet on balance, they are the most reliable methods we have for expanding knowledge and solving human problems. They have had a powerful effect in transforming world civilization. Wide sectors of the public today accept the utility of the sciences; they recognize that the sciences have had positive consequences.

    Unfortunately, the application of the methods of science is often confined to narrow specialties, and the broader implications of science to our view of reality are ignored. Humanists maintain that we need to extend the methods of science to other fields of human endeavor and that there should be no restrictions on scientific research, unless the research infringes on the rights of persons. Efforts to block free inquiry for moral, political, ideological, or religious reasons have invariably failed in the past. The possible beneficent results from continuous scientific discoveries cannot be underestimated.

- Second, *the opportunities that the sciences afford for expanding our knowledge of nature and human behavior are enormous.* Scientific naturalism presents a cosmic outlook based upon tested hypotheses and theories. It does not draw primarily upon religion, poetry, literature, or the arts for its account of reality—though these are important expressions of human interests. Scientific naturalists hold a form of nonreductive materialism; natural processes and events are best accounted for by reference to material causes. This form of naturalism leaves room for a pluralistic universe. Though nature is basically physical-chemical at root, processes and objects manifest themselves on many levels of observation: subatomic particles, atoms, and molecules; genes and cells; organisms, flowers, plants, and animals; psychological perception and cognition; social and cultural institutions; planets, stars, and galaxies. This allows for contextual explanations, drawing from the natural, biological, social and behavioral fields of inquiry. This does not deny the need to appreciate the various moral, aesthetic, and other cultural expressions of human experience.

• Third, *naturalists maintain that there is insufficient scientific evidence for spiritual interpretations of reality and the postulation of occult causes.* Classical transcendentalist doctrines no doubt expressed the passionate existential yearnings of human beings wishing to overcome death. The scientific theory of evolution, however, provides a more parsimonious account of human origins and is based upon evidence drawn from a wide range of sciences. We decry the efforts of a few scientists, often heralded by the mass media, to impose transcendental interpretations upon natural phenomena. Neither the standard modern cosmology nor the evolutionary process provides sufficient evidence for intelligent design, which is a leap of faith beyond the empirical evidence. We think it time for humanity to embrace its own adulthood—to leave behind the magical thinking and mythmaking that are substitutes for tested knowledge of nature.

IV
THE BENEFITS OF TECHNOLOGY

Humanists have consistently defended the beneficent value of scientific technology for human welfare. Philosophers from Francis Bacon to John Dewey have emphasized the increased power over nature that scientific knowledge affords and how it can contribute immeasurably to human advancement and happiness.

With the introduction of new technologies, unforeseen negative byproducts have often emerged. From the Luddites of the nineteenth century to the postmodernists of the twentieth century, critics have deplored the applications of technology. Humanists have long recognized that some technological innovations may engender problems. Unfortunately, technological applications, more often than not, are determined by economic considerations—by whether products are profitable—or by their military and political uses. There are vast dangers inherent in the *uncontrolled* use of technology. Weapons of mass destruction (thermonuclear, biological, and chemical) still have not been effectively regulated by the world community. Similarly, many breakthroughs in genetics, biology, and medical research (such as biogenetic engineering, cloning, organ transplant, and so forth) pose possible dangers, yet they offer enormous potentialities for human health and welfare.

Humanist Manifesto 2000

- First, *humanists strenuously object to efforts to limit technological research or to censor or restrict inquiry* a priori. It is difficult to predict beforehand where scientific research will lead or to forecast its possible benefits. We ought to be cautious about censoring such research.

- Second, *we hold that the best way to deal with issues concerning technological applications is by informed debate, not by appealing to absolutist dogma or emotional sloganeering.* Each technological innovation needs to be evaluated in terms of potential risk and potential benefit to society and the environment. It presupposes some level of scientific literacy.

- Third, *we cannot abandon technological solutions.* The economic and social structure of the contemporary world is becoming increasingly dependent upon technological innovation. If we are to solve our problems it will be not by retreating to an idyllic state of nature, but by developing new technologies that fulfill human needs and purposes, and doing so wisely and humanely.

- Fourth, *technological innovations that reduce overall human impact on the environment must be encouraged.*

- Fifth, *the spread of intermediate technologies that are affordable to the poor should be encouraged,* enabling them to benefit from the technological revolution.

V
ETHICS AND REASON

The realization of the highest ethical values is essential to the humanist outlook. We believe that the growth of scientific knowledge will enable humans to make wiser choices. In this way there is no impenetrable wall between *fact* and *value*, *is* and *ought*. Using reason and cognition will better enable us to appraise our values in the light of evidence and by their consequences.

Humanists have been unfairly accused of being unable to provide viable foundations for ethical responsibilities. Indeed, humanists are often blamed for the alleged moral breakdown of society. This argument is profoundly mistaken. Throughout the centuries philosophers have provided solid secular foundations for humanistic moral action. Moreover, countless millions of humanists have led exemplary lives, been responsible citizens, raised their children with loving care, and contributed significantly to the moral enhancement of society.

• Theological moral doctrines often reflect inherited, prescientific conceptions of nature and human nature. Contradictory moral commandments can be drawn from this legacy, and different religions frequently hold widely differing views on moral questions. Theists and transcendentalists have been both for and against slavery, the caste system, war, capital punishment, women's rights, and monogamy. Sectarian religionists have often slaughtered each other's adherents with impunity. Many of the terrible wars in the past and the present are inspired by intransigent religious dogmas. We do not deny that religionists have done much good; what we deny is that religious piety is the sole guarantee of moral virtue.

- Humanists everywhere have defended the separation of religion and state. We believe that the state should be *secular*, neither for nor against religion. We thus reject theocracies that seek to impose one moral or religious code on everyone. We believe that the state should allow a wide plurality of moral values to coexist.

- The basic principles of moral conduct are common to virtually all civilizations—whether religious or not. Moral tendencies are deeply rooted in human nature and have evolved throughout human history. Humanist ethics thus does not require agreement about theological or religious premises—we may never reach that—but it relates ethical choices ultimately to shared human interests, wants, needs, and values. We judge them by their consequences for human happiness and social justice. People of different sociocultural backgrounds do in fact apply similar general moral principles, though specific moral judgments may differ because of differing conditions. The challenge for societies thus is to emphasize our similarities, not our differences.

What are the key principles of the ethics of humanism?

- First, *the dignity and autonomy of the individual is the central value. Humanist ethics is committed to maximizing freedom of choice*: liberty of thought and conscience, the free mind and free inquiry, and the right of individuals to pursue their own lifestyles as they see fit so long as they do not harm others. This is especially relevant in democratic societies where there may be a multiplicity of alternative value systems. Humanists thus respect diversity.

- Second, *the humanist defense of individual self-determination does not mean that humanists condone just any kind of human conduct.* Nor does humanists' toleration of diverse lifestyles necessarily imply approval. Humanists insist that concomitant with the commitment to a free society is the constant need to raise the qualitative level of taste and appreciation. Humanists believe that freedom must be exercised responsibly. They recognize that all individuals live within communities and that some actions are destructive and wrong.

- Third, *humanist ethical philosophers have defended an ethic of excellence* (from Aristotle and Kant to John Stuart Mill, John Dewey, and M. N. Roy). Here some temperance, moderation, self-restraint, and self-control are present. Among the standards of excellence are the capacity for autonomous choice, creativity, aesthetic appreciation, mature motivation, rationality, and an obligation to fulfill one's highest talents. Humanism aims to bring out the best in people so that all people can have the best in life.

- Fourth, *humanists recognize our responsibilities and duties to others.* This means that we ought not to treat other human beings as mere objects for our own gratification; we must consider them as persons entitled to equality of consideration. Humanists hold that "each individual should be treated humanely." Similarly, they accept the Golden Rule that "we should not treat others as we would not like to be treated." They accept the biblical injunction that we should "accept the aliens within our midst," respecting their differences with us. Given the multiplicity of creeds, we are all strangers—yet can be friends—in the broader community.

- Fifth, humanists believe that the virtues of empathy and caring are essential for ethical conduct. This implies that we should develop an altruistic concern for the needs and interests of others. The foundations of moral conduct are the "common moral decencies"; that is, the general moral virtues that are widely shared by humans of diverse cultural and religious backgrounds: We ought to tell the truth, keep promises, be honest, sincere, beneficent, reliable, and dependable, show fidelity, appreciation, and gratitude; be fair-minded, just, and tolerant; we ought to negotiate our differences reasonably and try to be cooperative; we ought not to steal or to injure, maim, or harm other persons. Although humanists have called for liberation from repressive puritanical codes, they have likewise defended moral responsibility.

- Sixth, high on the humanist agenda is the need to provide moral education for children and young people, to develop character and an appreciation for the common moral decencies, and to encourage moral growth and the capacity for moral reasoning.

- Seventh, *humanists recommend that we use reason in framing our ethical judgments.* They point out that cognition is essential in formulating ethical choices. In particular, we need to engage in a process of deliberation if we are to resolve moral dilemmas. Human values and principles can best be justified in the light of reflective inquiry. Where differences exist we need to negotiate them wherever we can by rational dialogue.

- Eighth, *humanists maintain that we should be prepared to modify ethical principles and values in the light of current realities and future expectations.* We need to draw upon the best moral wisdom of the past, but also to develop new solutions for moral dilemmas, whether old or new.

  For example, the debate over voluntary euthanasia has intensified particularly in affluent societies, because medical technology now enables us to keep terminally ill patients alive who might earlier have died. Humanists have argued for death with dignity and the right of competent adults to refuse medical treatment, reducing unnecessary suffering and even hastening death. They have also recognized the importance of the hospice movement in easing the dying process.

  Likewise, we should be prepared to select rationally

the new reproductive powers made possible by scientific research—such as *in vitro* fertilization, surrogate motherhood, genetic engineering, organ transplantation, and cloning. We cannot look back to the moral absolutes of the past for guidance here. We need to respect autonomy of choice.

- Ninth, *humanists argue that we should respect an ethic of principles.* This means that the end does not justify the means; on the contrary, our ends are shaped by our means, and there are limits to what we are permitted to do. This is especially important today in light of the tyrannical dictatorships of the twentieth century, in which political ideologies held with near-religious zeal compromised moral means to achieve visionary ends. We are keenly aware of the tragic suffering inflicted on millions by those willing to condone great evil in pursuit of a supposed greater good.

VI
A UNIVERSAL COMMITMENT
TO HUMANITY AS A WHOLE

The overriding need of the world community today is to develop a new Planetary Humanism—one that seeks to preserve human rights and enhance human freedom and dignity, but also emphasizes our *commitment to humanity as a whole.*

- First, *the underlying ethical principle of Planetary Humanism is the need to respect the dignity and worth of all persons in the world community.* No doubt each person already recognizes multiple responsibilities relative to his or her social context: persons have responsibilities to family, friends, the community, city, state, or nation in which they reside. We need, however, to add to these responsibilities a new commitment that has emerged—our responsibility to persons beyond our national boundaries. Now, more than ever, we are linked morally and physically to each person on the globe, and the bell tolls for all when it tolls for one.

- Second, *we ought to act so as to mitigate human suffering and to increase the sum of human happiness* wherever it is possible to do so, and this responsibility extends to the whole world. This principle is recognized by both religious believers and nonbelievers. It is essential to the entire framework of human morality. No community can long endure if it condones wholesale violations of the common moral decencies among its own members. The key question today concerns the range of the principle. We submit that this moral duty should be generalized: we should be concerned not only with the well-being of those within our community or nation-state but also with the entire world community.

- Third, *we should avoid an overemphasis on multicultural parochialism, which can be divisive and destructive.* We should be tolerant of cultural diversity except where those cultures are themselves intolerant or repressive. It is time to rise above narrow tribalism to find common ground. Ethnicities are the result of past social and geographical isolations that are no longer relevant in an open global society where interaction and intermarriage among different ethnicities are not only possible, but are to be encouraged. Although loyalty to one's own country, tribe, or ethnic group can take individuals beyond selfish interests, excessive chauvinism among ethnic groups and nation-states frequently becomes destructive. Moral caring and loyalty thus should not end at ethnic enclaves or national frontiers. A rational morality enjoins us to build and support institutions of cooperation among individuals of different ethnicities. It would integrate, not separate us from one another.

- Fourth, *respect and concern for persons should apply to all human beings equally.* This in turn means that all human beings should be treated humanely and that we should defend human rights everywhere. Accordingly, each of us has a duty to help mitigate the suffering of people anywhere in the world and to contribute to the common good. This principle expresses our highest sense of compassion and benevolence. It implies that people living in the affluent nations have an obligation to mitigate suffering and enhance the well-being, where they can, of people in the impoverished regions of the world. Likewise, it means that those in the less-developed regions have an obligation to replace resentment against the affluent with reciprocal goodwill. The best that the affluent can do for the poor is to help them to help themselves. If the poorer members of the human family are to be helped, the affluent may have to limit their own wasteful consumption and excessive self-indulgence.

- Fifth, *these principles should apply not only to the world community of the present time, but also to the future.* We have a responsibility to posterity—both in the immediate future and on a longer time scale. Rational ethical persons thus recognize their extended obligation to our children's children's offspring and to the community of all human beings, present and future.

- Sixth, *each generation has an obligation, as far as possible, to leave the planetary environment that it inherits a better place.* We should avoid excessive pollution, and we should use what we need rationally and sparingly to avoid wasting the earth's nonrenewable resources. At a time of rapid population growth and accelerating consumption of resources, this may seem an impossible ideal. But we must try, for our actions today will determine the fate of generations yet to come. We can look back and retrospectively evaluate the actions of our forebears, and we can praise or blame them for their acts of omission or commission. We can criticize, for example, those who depleted oil and natural-gas reserves with abandon, or exhausted water supplies. Conversely, we can thank the architects and engineers of the past for the natural preserves, fine water-treatment plants, underground disposal systems, highways, and bridges that they built and which we use today.

We can empathize with the future world and imaginatively project what those who will live then will be like, and we can infer obligations today for those tomorrow. Our obligation to the future stems in part from our gratitude, or perhaps condemnation, of generations previous to ours and the sacrifices that they made from which we benefit. Future generations need spokespersons today, serving as their proxies and defending their future rights. To so argue is not to impose an impossible obligation, because a good portion of the human race already is morally concerned about future posterity, including a concern for the environment. One may even argue that the heroic idealism devoted to a beloved cause beyond themselves and for the greater good of humanity has always inspired human beings.

- Seventh, *we should take care to do nothing that would endanger the very survival of future generations.* We must see to it that our planetary society does not so degrade the atmosphere, waters, and soil that life in the future would be drastically undermined. We should see to it that our planetary society does not unleash weapons of mass destruction. For the first time in history humankind possesses the means to destroy itself. The present abatement of the Cold War is no guarantee that the ultimate sword of Damocles will not be dropped by fanatical disciples of vengeance or by those whose brinkmanship would allow the world to be destroyed in order to save it.

Thus, a viable new Planetary Humanism focusing on a safe, secure, and better world should be our overriding obligation, and we should do what we can to engender ethical commitment. This commitment should apply to all people on the planet, whether religious or naturalistic, theist or humanist, rich or poor, of whatever race, ethnicity, or nationality.

We need to convince our fellow human beings about the imperative to work together in creating a new planetary consensus in which preserving and improving the lot of humanity as a whole is our supreme obligation.

VII
A PLANETARY BILL OF RIGHTS
AND RESPONSIBILITIES

To fulfill our commitment to Planetary Humanism, we propose *A Planetary Bill of Rights and Responsibilities*, the embodiment of our planetary commitment to the well-being of humanity as a whole. It incorporates the *Universal Declaration of Human Rights*, but goes beyond it by offering some new provisions. Many independent countries have sought to implement these provisions within their own national borders. But there is a growing need for an explicit *Planetary Bill of Rights and Responsibilities* that applies to all members of the human species. Its implementation will not be easy. It is contingent, of course, on there being sufficient resources. Although the free market is a dynamic engine of economic growth and development, it is not infallible, and it may need to be supplemented by public policies concerned with the broader social good. The means adopted to achieve the *Bill*'s principles will most likely draw primarily upon the private sector, but the public sector has a role to play as well. There will no doubt be tremendous political opposition to these proposals, but we should at least set long-range goals, even though they may be presently difficult to achieve in certain parts of the world.

- First, *we should strive to end poverty and malnutrition and to provide adequate health care and shelter for people everywhere on the planet.* This means that nobody should be denied adequate food and clean water and we should try our best to eradicate infectious diseases, ensure proper sanitation, and guarantee a minimum standard of housing for everyone. This is quite a task; yet on moral grounds it is imperative that we begin to undertake this work.

- Second, *we should strive to provide economic security and adequate income for everyone.* This means giving people a fair chance for employment, unemployment insurance, and social security for retirement. There should be special programs to educate the handicapped in skills for which they are capable and to help them find employment.

    The central premise here is self-help: that individuals need to exert their own efforts to earn sufficient income. All that society can do is provide opportunities—by private or public means.

- Third, *every person should be protected from unwarranted and unnecessary injury, danger, and death.* Every member of the human species should be secure from physical violence, theft of personal property, and fear due to intimidation (whether by private persons or social or political institutions). They should be protected from sexual abuse, harassment, and rape. Sexual conduct should be based on the principle of consent. Sex with or marriage to children should not be permitted under any circumstances.

    Capital punishment is an inadmissible form of retribution. It should be replaced by other deterrents, such as life imprisonment. Most civilized nations have already prohibited the death penalty.

• Fourth, *individuals should have the right to live in a family unit or household of their choice, consonant with their income, and should have the right to bear or not to bear children.* Every individual should have the right to freely choose life partners, if any, and the number and spacing of their children. Persons should have the right to raise their biological or adopted children, or not to have families.

Those who elect to raise children have certain requirements incumbent upon them: Parents should provide a secure and loving environment for their children. Children should not be abused by parents. Young children and adolescents should not be compelled into adult labor or excessive drudgery. Parents should not neglect their children or deny them proper nutrition, sanitation, shelter, medical care, and safety.

Parents should not deny their children access to education, cultural enrichment, and intellectual stimulation. Although parental moral guidance is vital, parents should not simply impose their own religious outlook or moral values on their children or indoctrinate them. Children, adolescents, and young adults should have exposure to different viewpoints and enjoy encouragement to think for themselves. The views of even young children should be respected.

- Fifth, *the opportunity for education and cultural enrichment should be universal.* Every person should have the opportunity to expand his or her knowledge. As a minimum, schooling should be made available for every child from the earliest years through adolescence. But the opportunity for education should be made available to all age groups, including continuing education for adults. There are minimum standards that every person should attain: the basic skills of reading, writing, mathematics. Higher levels of attainment relate to talent and capacity. Admission to schools of higher education should be based on merit; where possible, scholarships should be granted so that no qualified student must forsake educational opportunity because of financial straits.

- All children should be taught some basic marketable skills, to ensure them the possibility of gainful employment. This should include some form of computer literacy, cultural edification, and the ability to function in the world of commerce.

  The curriculum should promote an understanding of scientific methods of inquiry and critical thinking. No limits should be placed on free inquiry. Education should include an appreciation of the natural, biological, and social sciences. The theory of evolution and the standards of ecology should also be studied.

  Students should learn the principles of good health, adequate nutrition, sanitation, and exercise. Included in these should be some understanding of scientific medicine and how the human body functions. The opportunity for appropriate sexual education should be made available from an early age. This should include responsible sexual behavior, family planning, and contraceptive techniques.

Students should learn to appreciate diverse cultural traditions. This should include the comparative study of religions, languages, and cultures, and an appreciation for artistic expression. Students should study history beginning with the history of the particular country or culture in which they live, but should also study other cultures, including the history of world civilizations. Every effort should be made to develop "planetary literacy," i.e., environmental awareness. Learning should not be confined to narrow specialties, but some effort at interdisciplinary understanding should be encouraged.

- Sixth, *individuals should not be discriminated against because of race, ethnic origin, nationality, culture, caste, class, creed, gender, or sexual orientation.* We need to develop a new human identity—membership in the planetary community. This identity must have priority over all others and can serve as the basis for eradicating discrimination.

- Racial, national, and ethnic hatred are immoral. All individuals are members of the same species and as such should be entitled to enjoy all the privileges and opportunities available.

- Class antagonism can be a source of discrimination. Traditional barriers, such as the caste system, have held back millions from advancement. Some have sought to close the gap between rich and poor by impoverishing the former instead of improving conditions for the latter. Others have ignored the plight of the poor or sought to keep them in a state of dependency.

• The right to believe and practice one's religion or belief without discrimination must be respected. The equivalent freedom, not to practice religion, should be afforded to religious dissenters, agnostics, and atheists, whose views deserve no lesser respect.

• Gender discrimination should not be permitted. Women have a right to be treated equally with men. Discrimination in job opportunity, education, or cultural activities is insupportable. Society should not deny homosexuals, bisexuals, or transgendered and transsexuals equal rights.

• Seventh, *the principles of equality should be respected by civilized communities, and in four major senses*:

  • *Equality before the law*: Every person should be afforded due process and equal protection of the laws. The same laws must apply to government officials as well as to ordinary citizens. No one should be above the law. Laws should be blind to race, color, ethnicity, creed, sex, and wealth.

  • *Equality of consideration*: Every person has equal dignity and value and shall not be denied benefits and rights accorded all others. This does not deny society the right to restrain, punish, or incarcerate individuals who break the law, use violence, or commit crimes against others.

- *Satisfaction of basic needs*: Individuals may lack resources and through no fault of their own be unable to satisfy their minimal needs for food, shelter, safety, health care, cultural enrichment, and education. In such cases, if society has the means, then it has an obligation to help satisfy as many of these basic needs as possible. This welfare concern is related to the ability to work. Society should not encourage a culture of dependency.

- *Equality of opportunity*: In free societies there should be a level playing field. In an open and free society, adults and children should be afforded the opportunities to fulfill their interests and aspirations, and to express their unique talents.

- Eighth, *it is the right of every person to be able to live a good life, pursue happiness, achieve creative satisfaction and leisure in his or her own terms, so long as he or she does not harm others.* The core principle is that each person should be afforded the opportunity to realize his or her own personal fulfillment, concomitant with social resources, but this actual realization depends on the individual and not on society. Happiness, however, is dependent upon a person's own income, resources, and attitudes, and individuals should not expect society to provide the means of satisfaction for a wide range of idiosyncratic tastes and pursuits.

- Ninth, *individuals should have the opportunity to appreciate and participate in the arts*–including literature, poetry, drama, sculpture, dance, music, and song. Aesthetic imagination and creative activities can contribute immeasurably to the enrichment of life, self-realization, and human happiness. Society should encourage and support the arts and their wide cultural dissemination to all sectors of the community.

- Tenth, *individuals should not be unduly restrained, restricted, or prohibited from exercising a wide range of personal choices.* This includes freedom of thought and conscience–the unqualified right to believe, or not to believe, freedom of speech and freedom to pursue one's own lifestyle, so long as one does not prevent others from exercising their rights.

  - Included in the above is *the right to privacy*:

    - The confidentiality of individuals should be respected.

    - Every individual should be free from intrusive political or social coercion.

    - Women should have the right to control their own bodies. This includes reproductive freedom, voluntary contraception, and abortion.

- Couples should have proper information for family planning and the ability to avail themselves of artificial insemination and biogenetic counseling.

- Adults should be allowed to marry whomever they wish, even if of different racial, ethnic, religious, class, caste, or national background. Miscegenation should not be prohibited. Same-sex couples should have the same rights as heterosexual couples.

- Informed consent should be the guiding principle of health care. Mature individuals should have the right to select or reject medical treatment.

- Individuals should have the right to join voluntary organizations in order to share common interests and activities. The right of free association, so long as it is peaceful and nonviolent, must be respected.

VIII
A NEW GLOBAL AGENDA

Many of the high ideals that emerged following the Second World War, and that found expression in such instruments as the *Universal Declaration of Human Rights*, have waned throughout the world. If we are to influence the future of humankind, we will need to work increasingly with and through the new centers of power and influence to improve equity and stability, alleviate poverty, reduce conflict, and safeguard the environment. In light of these changing circumstances a number of priority objectives have become apparent:

• First, *security*: The problem of regional conflicts and wars has not been resolved, nor has the lurking danger posed by weapons of mass destruction. In the past fifty years intercommunal violence and civil war have far exceeded conflicts among nations both in terms of number and human cost. Such conflicts invariably arise when one ethnic community within a state feels oppressed by the government or by another community, and feels unable to express its grievances by legal means. The United Nations Charter specifically prohibits interference in the internal affairs of a member state; the international community therefore lacks any legal basis for attempts to resolve tribal, ethnic, or intercommunal conflict within national boundaries against the wishes of the governing group in the state concerned. Furthermore, any attempt by the international community to resolve such conflicts by the use of force is likely to be met in the UN Security Council by the veto of a permanent member friendly to the government concerned. Since the end of the Cold War, the United States, supported by NATO and the other Western powers, has often sought to impose peace by force, bypassing the United Nations and seriously undermining its authority.

* Second, *human development.* We call for daring and innovative proposals to maximize human progress on the global scale. The disparity between the affluent and the underdeveloped sectors of the planet is an urgent problem today as in the past. The developed world can help to overcome it in part by providing capital, technical aid, and educational assistance.

We need a new emphasis on social, not simply economic, development, recognizing that while economic development does not always lead to social development, direct investment in social development can reduce poverty and bring more people into the money economy. There is a need to support measures that will directly benefit the health and well being of the poorest, and especially of women and girls. This must include some efforts to stabilize and then decrease population-growth rates.

Development assistance has frequently been seen by donor countries as an instrument of foreign imperialism and trade policy. With the end of the Cold War the perceived need to compete for the support of the developing world has diminished, and with it the scale of development assistance. This trend must be reversed.

We urge all industrialized nations to accept as a first step the guidelines set out by the United Nations for overseas development assistance, namely to contribute (or be taxed) 0.7 percent of their GNP each year to development assistance, of which 20 percent should be for social development, and with 20 percent of the social development budget being allocated to population assistance. This assistance should be increased in future years.

More effort must be given to bridging the knowledge gap in the poorest nations, to training and retraining for the unemployed, to providing better working conditions (especially for women and the underprivileged), and to allocating more resources to health care, education, and cultural enrichment.

We urge all nations to support the 1994 "Cairo Programme of Action" to provide universal reproductive health and reproductive rights, to help improve the quality of life of the poorest, and to stabilize world population growth. The Human Development Index published annually by the United Nations Development Programme should be promoted as a measure of social performance for every developing country.

There is an increasing role for nongovernmental organizations (NGOs) in developing countries to act as direct recipients of development assistance in order to short-cut the corruption and bureaucratic delays endemic in many such countries. Western nongovernmental organizations have a significant role to play as partners and as channels for such development assistance.

- Third, *social justice*: *The Planetary Bill of Rights and Responsibilities* is central to questions of social justice. Attempts to qualify the impact of social justice or to restrict its geographical or cultural scope must be resisted. The applicability of the *Declaration of Human Rights* to the private sphere of home, family, and community must be reemphasized. We especially urge the early ratification by all countries of all the international conventions on the rights of women, children, minorities, and indigenous peoples.

- Fourth, *the growth of global conglomerates*: The past twenty years have witnessed an increasing concentration of power and wealth in the hands of global corporations. No doubt they have contributed to world trade and economic development. Yet international law has been slow to respond to the rapidly evolving power structures in the world economy. Multinational corporations are now largely able to disregard the wishes of individual governments in formulating policy, moving financial resources across boundaries, and exporting manufacturing to the cheapest market. This freedom is seen as beneficial to the free market and is encouraged by global financial markets. But such corporations are also largely able to avoid taxes by exporting profits. Financial institutions are able to evade financial control by basing their structures in offshore tax havens, while international fund transfers approaching a trillion dollars per day go untaxed. Wealthy individuals are similarly able to avoid paying their fair share of taxes.

Any proposal to address these issues but that would restrict the operation of the free market would be strenuously resisted and would certainly fail. Imaginative reforms are therefore needed to ensure that the international wealthy, both corporations and individuals, pay their fair share without damaging the engine of the world economy.

- Fifth, *international law*: The global community needs to develop a system of international law that transcends the laws of the separate nations. We need to transform a lawless world into one that has laws everyone can understand and abide by.

- Sixth, *the environment*: We need to recognize that current lifestyles in the industrialized North are unsustainable and will become increasingly so as economic development and increasing consumption in the poorer nations of the South increase pressure on the global environment. Runaway consumption is already putting unprecedented pressure on the environment and placing those who consume the least in double jeopardy. The problem is to raise the consumption levels of the one billion poorest who lack even one adequate meal a day while simultaneously implementing more sustainable consumption patterns that reduce environmental damage.

Global environmental problems must be dealt with at the planetary level: reducing environmental pollution, including carbon dioxide and other greenhouse gases; developing alternative fuels; reforesting denuded lands; counteracting the erosion of topsoil in cultivable areas; facilitating environmentally friendly businesses; limiting fishing on the high seas that threatens the extinction of entire fish populations; protecting endangered species; reducing the addictive lifestyle of conspicuous wasteful consumption; and banning all weapons of mass destruction. Measures to protect the environment thus need high priority for the planetary community.

IX
THE NEED FOR NEW
PLANETARY INSTITUTIONS

The urgent question in the twenty-first century is whether humankind can develop global institutions to address these problems. Many of the best remedies are those adopted on the local, national, and regional level by voluntary, private, and public efforts. One strategy is to seek solutions through free-market initiatives; another is to use international voluntary foundations and organizations for educational and social development. We believe, however, that there remains a need to develop new global institutions that will deal with the problems directly and will focus on the needs of humanity as a whole.

In the aftermath of the Second World War a number of international institutions, such as the United Nations and the World Health Organization, were founded to deal with these tasks. Unfortunately, a wide gap has appeared between the way in which these institutions operate and the needs of the new planetary community. Existing institutions must therefore change dramatically, or new institutions must be forged.

The *de facto* political boundaries of the world are arbitrary. We need to go beyond them. We need to continue to defend the growth of democracy in the diverse nations in the world community, but we also need to enhance the transnational rights of all members of the planetary community. *We need now more than ever a world body that represents the* people *of the world rather than nation-states.*

The United Nations, unlike its precursor, the League of Nations, has played a vital role in the world, but there is so much more that still needs to be accomplished. To solve problems on the transnational level and to contribute to planetwide development, we need gradually but drastically to transform the United Nations. Some of these changes will involve amending the UN Charter; others will entail radically altering the structure of the UN; these changes will require the consent of the member nations. But whatever alterations ensue, we should preserve those elements in the UN that have so dramatically improved the lives of millions on the planet.

The most fundamental change would be to enhance the effectiveness of the UN by converting it from an assembly of sovereign states to an assembly of peoples as well. Such a transformation does have precedents, including the self-conversion of America's early confederation of sovereign states into the current federal system. If we are to solve our global problems, nation-states must transfer some of their sovereignty to a system of transnational authority. Failure to do so will risk having the world locked in conflict among sovereign states whose primary interest is sovereignty. We can scarcely afford such a waste of resources; the world's people deserve better. Such a transnational system would no doubt engender opposition from political leaders everywhere—especially nationalist-chauvinists. But it could still evolve—and succeed—if we work for a planetary ethical consensus.

Any new transnational system should be democratic and would have limited powers. There would be a maximization of autonomy, decentralization, and freedom for the independent states and regions of the world. There would also have to be a system of checks and balances as a safeguard against arbitrary power. The transnational system would deal primarily with questions that can only be solved on the global level, such as security, the defense of human rights, economic and social development, and the protection of the planetary environment. If these goals are to be achieved, then we offer the following reforms, working from the framework of the United Nations:

- First, *the world needs at some point in the future to establish an effective World Parliament—and elections to it based on population—which will represent the people, not their governments.* The idea of a World Parliament is similar to the evolution of the European Parliament, still in its infancy. The current UN General Assembly is an assembly of nations. This new World Parliament would enact legislative policies in a democratic manner. Perhaps a bicameral legislature is the most feasible with both a Parliament of peoples and a General Assembly of nations. The detailed formal structure can only be worked out by a charter review convention that we recommend should be convened to examine thoroughly options for strengthening the UN and/or supplementing it with a parliamentary system.

- Second, *the world needs a workable security system to resolve military conflicts that threaten the peace. We need to amend the*

United Nations Charter to achieve this aim. Thus the veto in the Security Council by the Big Five needs to be repealed. It exists because of historical circumstances at the end of World War II that are no longer relevant. The basic principle of world security is that no single state or alliance of states has the right to undermine the political and territorial integrity of other states by aggression; nor should any nation or group of nations be allowed to police the world or unilaterally bomb others without the concurrence of the Security Council. The world needs an effective police force to protect regions of the world from conflict and to negotiate peaceful settlements. We recommend that the UN Security Council, elected by the General Assembly and World Parliament, should require a three-quarter vote to take any security measures. This would mean that if the current fifteen-member Council were retained, then if four or more members disagreed, no action could be taken.

- Third, *we must develop an effective World Court and an International Judiciary with sufficient power to enforce its rulings.* The World Court in The Hague is already moving in this direction. This Court will have the power to try violations of human rights, genocide, and transnational crimes and to adjudicate conflicting international disputes. It is essential that those states that do not as yet recognize its authority be persuaded to do so.

- Fourth, *the world needs a planetary environmental monitoring agency on the transnational level.* We recommend the strengthening of existing UN agencies and programs most directly concerned with the environment. The United Nations Environment Programme, for example, should be given the power to enforce measures against serious ecological pollution. The United Nations Population Fund must be allocated sufficient funding to satisfy the unmet global need for contraception and therefore help stabilize population growth. Should these agencies prove unable to cope with the massive problems, a stronger planetary agency will need to be created.

• Fifth, *we recommend an international system of taxation in order to assist the underdeveloped sectors of the human family and to fulfill social needs not fulfilled by market forces.* We would begin with a tax levied on the Gross National Product (GNP) of *all* nations, the proceeds to be used for economic and social assistance and development. This would not be a voluntary contribution but an actual tax. The existing vital agencies of the United Nations would be financed by the funds raised. This includes UNESCO, UNICEF, the World Health Organization, the World Bank, the International Monetary Fund, and other organizations.

Wide international agreement on tax reform is needed to ensure that multinational corporations pay their fair share of the global tax burden. Tax credits should be given for charitable donations for human and social development. A levy on international fund transfers should be seriously considered to tax otherwise untaxed funds and to help finance social development in the poorest countries. Many member states refuse to pay their dues to the UN. For these states censure and stronger measures such as sanctions should be imposed. The selective cancellations of burdensome debts by poor countries unable to pay should be financed by this fund.

- Sixth, *the development of global institutions should include some procedure for the regulation of multinational corporations and state monopolies.* This goes beyond existing UN mandates. We should encourage free-market economies, yet we cannot ignore the planetary needs of humanity as a whole. If left unchecked, mega-corporations and monopolies are likely to impair human rights, the environment, and the prosperity of certain regions of the world. Extreme disparities between the affluent and the under-developed sectors of the planet can be overcome by encouraging self-help, but also by harnessing the wealth of the world to provide capital, technical aid, and educational assistance for economic and social development.

- Seventh, *we must keep alive a free market of ideas, respect diversity of opinion, and cherish the right to dissent.* There is thus a special compelling need to resist control of the media of communication, whether by national governments, by powerful economic interests, or by global institutions. Dictatorships have used the media for propagandistic purposes, denying alternative viewpoints. The mass media in capitalist societies are often under oligopolic control. These media often pander to the lowest common denominator in order to maximize ratings. Facts are disregarded in the uncritical acceptance of any New Age quackery, while reports of miracles gain more air time than the latest scientific breakthrough. Many media–TV, radio, films, publishing–apparently feel little obligation to provide factual or educational content.

We eschew any form of censorship, whether practiced by governments, advertisers, or media proprietors. Competition in the media, by the creation of public and not-for-profit media organizations, should be encouraged and all movement toward monopoly and oligarchical control should be resisted. Popular voluntary movements to monitor the media and to publicize their more blatant excesses should be encouraged. There is a special need to keep open access to the media of communication. This means that neither powerful global media oligopolies nor nation-states should dominate the media. We need to mount a democratic movement worldwide to allow for cultural diversity and enrichment and a free give-and-take of ideas.

X
OPTIMISM ABOUT THE
HUMAN PROSPECT

Finally, and perhaps most important, as members of the human community on this planet we need to nurture a sense of optimism about the Human Prospect. Although many problems may seem intractable, we have good reasons to believe that we can marshal our best talents to solve them, and that by goodwill and dedication a better life is attainable by more and more members of the human community. Planetary Humanism holds forth great promises for humankind. We wish to cultivate a sense of wonder and excitement about the potential opportunities for realizing enriched lives for ourselves and for generations yet to be born. Ideals are progenitors of the future. We will not succeed unless we resolve to do so; and we will not resolve to do so unless we have confidence that we can. Any optimism that we generate should be based upon a realistic appraisal of the possibilities of achievement, yet we need to be motivated by the belief that we can overcome adversity.

Planetary Humanism rejects nihilistic philosophies of doom and despair and those that counsel an escape from reason and freedom, that fester in fear and foreboding, and that are obsessed with apocalyptic scenarios of Armageddon. The human species has always faced challenges. That is the continuing saga of our planetary adventure. As humanists we urge today, as in the past, that humans not look beyond themselves for salvation. We alone are responsible for our own destiny, and the best we can do is to muster our intelligence, courage, and compassion to realize our highest aspirations. We believe that a good life is possible for each and every person of the planetary society of the future. Life can be meaningful for those willing to assume responsibility and undertake the cooperative efforts necessary to fulfill its promise. We can and ought to help create the new world of tomorrow. The future can be wholesome and bountiful, and it can open up new, daring, and exciting vistas. Planetary Humanism can contribute significantly to the development of the positive attitudes so necessary if we are to realize the unparalleled opportunities that await humankind in the third millennium and beyond.

Those who sign this document earnestly seek partnership with the diverse world cultures, including the major religious traditions of the world. We believe it urgent that we strive for common ground and that we seek shared values. We need to enter into continued give-and-take—not simply with those who agree with us, but with those who may differ. In the midst of our diversity and the plurality of our traditions, we need to recognize that we are all part of an extended human family, sharing a common planetary habitat. The very success of our species now threatens the future of human existence. We alone are responsible for our collective destiny. Solving our problems will require the cooperation and wisdom of all members of the world community. It is within the power of each human being to make a difference. The planetary community is our own, and each of us can help make it flourish. The future is open. The choices are for us to make. Together we can realize the noblest ends and ideals of humankind.

Those who endorse *Humanist Manifesto 2000* do not necessarily agree with every provision in it. We do, however, accept its main principles and offer it in order to contribute to constructive dialogue. We invite other men and women representing different traditions to join with us in working for a better world in the planetary society that is now emerging.

ENDORSED BY THE FOLLOWING DISTINGUISHED INDIVIDUALS*

ARGENTINA

HUGO DANIEL ESTRELLA, Pugwash Conference

AUSTRALIA

PHILLIP ADAMS, columnist, commentator, Australian Broadcast Network

JOHN ARTHUR PASSMORE, professor of historical studies, Australian National University; former president, Academy of Sciences

J.J. C. SMART, professor emeritus, Australian National University

BANGLADESH

TASLIMA NASRIN, author, Human Rights Advocate

BELGIUM

JEAN DOMMANGET, Observatoire Royal de Belgique, Brussels

---

*Institutions for identification only.

BRAZIL

JOSÉ LEITE LOPES, professor emeritus, Centro Brasileiro de Pesquisas Físicas

CANADA

MARIO BUNGE, professor emeritus, Foundations and Philosophy of Science Unit, McGill University
ROBERT BUCKMAN, M.D.
HENRY MORGENTALER, M.D., abortion rights activist
MARVIN ZAYED, author

CHINA

YOUZHENG LI, Institute of Philosophy, Beijing

COLOMBIA

RUBEN ARDILA, professor of psychology, National University of Colombia, Bogota

COSTA RICA

ANGEL RUIZ, director, Center of Mathematics and Meta-Mathematics, University of Costa Rica

CROATIA

RADOVAN VUKADINOVIĆ, director, graduate program in international relations, University of Zagreb

DENMARK

JENS C. SKOU, Nobel laureate, biophysicist, University of Aarhus

EGYPT

MOURAD WAHBA, president, Averroës and the Enlightenment International Association; founder, Afro-Asian Philosophy Association

FRANCE

ETIENNE BAULIEU, discoverer of RU486, Academy of Sciences, INSERM

R. M. BONNET, European Space Agency

JACQUES BOUVERESSE, professor of philosophy, Collège de France

JEAN-PIERRE CHANGEUX, professor of neurobiology, Collège de France; Neurological Molecular Laboratory, Institut Pasteur

GÉRARD FUSSMAN, professor, Collège de France, Paris

YVES GALIFRET, professor emeritus, Institut des Neurosciences, Université Pierre et Marie Curie

JACQUES LE GOFF, specialist in medieval French civilization and literature, ENESS

JEAN-MARIE LEHN, Nobel laureate, Université Louis Pasteur

JEAN-CLAUDE PECKER, astronomer, Collège de France; Academy of Sciences

EVRY SCHATZMAN, astronomer, former president, French Physics Association; Academy of Sciences

GERMANY

WERNER SCHULTZ, editor, *Diesseits*

GREECE

DENNIS V. RAZIS, M.D., The Delphi Society, Athens

INDIA

G. R. R. BABU, executive director, International Humanist and Ethical Union

PUSHPA MITTRA BHARGAVA, founding director, Centre for Cellular and Molecular Biology, Hyderabad

AMLAN DATTA, former vice chancellor, Visva Bharati

SANAL EDAMARUKU, secretary general, Indian Rationalist Association, New Delhi

NARISETTI INNAIAH, professor of philosophy; chair, Committee of Child Abuse

H. NARASIMHAIAH, president, Bangalore Science Forum, National College

INDUMATI PARIKH, director, M. N. Roy Human Development Centre

AVULA SAMBASIVA RAO, former chief justice, Andhra Pradesh; former vice president, Andhra University

SIBNARAYAN RAY, Raja Rammohun Roy Library Foundation

V. M. TARKUNDE, senior advocate, Supreme Court

RAVIPUDI VENKATADRI, editor, *Hetuvadi*

KENYA

RICHARD LEAKEY, anthropologist, Kenya Wildlife Service

NEPAL

GANGA PRASAD SUBEDI, secretary, Humanist Association of Nepal

GOPI UPRETI, president, Humanist Association of Nepal

NETHERLANDS

PIETER V. ADMIRAAL, M.D.

MAX ROOD, professor of law, Rijksuniversiteit te Leiden; former minister of justice

ROB A. P. TIELMAN, professor of sociology, University of Utrecht

NEW ZEALAND

WILLIAM COOKE, lecturer, Manakau Institute of Technology

NORWAY

LEVI FRAGELL, president, IHEU

BERNT HAGTVET, department of political science, University of Oslo

TOVE BEATE PEDERSEN, secretary general, Norwegian Humanist Association

POLAND

BARBARA STANOSZ, professor of philosophy, Warsaw University; editor, *Bez Dogmatu*

RUSSIA

GARRY I. ABELEV, N. N. Blokhin Cancer Research Center

YURI NIKOLAEVICH EFREMOV, department head, Sternberg Astronomical Institute, Moscow State University

VITALIĬ GINZBURG, physicist, academician, Academy of Sciences

GIVI GIVISHVILI, IZMIRAN: Institute of Terrestrial Magnetism, Ionosphere and Radiowave Propagation

SERGEĬ KAPITZA, Institue for Physical Problems

VALERIĬ KUVAKIN, professor of Russian philosophy, Moscow State University

NIKITA MOISEEV, professor of mathematics

ALEXANDER V. RAZIN, professor of ethics, Moscow State University

SPAIN

JOSÉ M. R. DELGADO, professor of neurobiology, Centro de Estudios Neurobiologicos

JOSÉ SARAMAGO, Nobel laureate

ALBERTO HIDALGO TUÑÓN, professor of the sociology of knowledge, Universidad de Oviedo; Sociedad Asturiana de Filosofía

SRI LANKA

SIR ARTHUR C. CLARKE, CBE, author; chancellor, University of Moratuwa; chancellor, International Space University

SWEDEN

GEORGE KLEIN, professor and research-group leader, Microbiology and Tumorbiology Center, Karolinska Institute

SWITZERLAND

DIANA BROWN, representative of IHEU at the UN in Geneva

ROY W. BROWN, founder, World Population Foundation

JACK STEINBERGER, Nobel laureate, physicist, CERN

SYRIA

SADIK AL AZM, professor of philosophy, University of
Damascus

UNITED KINGDOM

COLIN BLAKEMORE, University Laboratory of Physiology,
Oxford

BERNARD CRICK, professor emeritus of politics, Birkbeck
College, London University

RICHARD DAWKINS, New College, Oxford

LORD LIONEL ELVIN, House of Lords

SIR RAYMOND FIRTH, professor of anthropology, University of London

JIM HERRICK, editor, *New Humanist*; Rationalist Press
Association

TED HONDERICH, Grote professor emeritus of the philosophy of mind and logic, University College London

SIR HAROLD W. KROTO, Nobel laureate, School of Chemistry, Physics and Environmental Science

ANWAR SHAIKH, author

HARRY STOPES-ROE, professor of philosophy, University
of Birmingham

HAZHIR TEIMOURIAN, writer and broadcaster

POLLY TOYNBEE, columnist, *The Guardian*

JANE WYNNE WILLSON, former president, British Humanist Association

LEWIS WOLPERT, professor of anatomy, University College of London

USA

NORM ALLEN JR., director, African Americans for Humanism

STEVE ALLEN, author, entertainer

DEREK ARAUJO, president, Campus Freethought Alliance

KHOREN ARISIAN, minister emeritus, First Unitarian Society of Minneapolis

KURT BAIER, professor emeritus of philosophy, University of Pittsburgh

ROBERT A. BAKER, professor of psychology, University of Kentucky

JOSEPH E. BARNHART, professor of philosophy and religious studies, University of North Texas

BARUJ BENACERRAF, Nobel laureate, Dana-Farber Cancer Institute

H. JAMES BIRX, professor of anthropology, Canisius College

JO ANN BOYDSTON, distinguished professor emerita, Southern Illinois University

PAUL D. BOYER, Nobel laureate in chemistry

GWEN W. BREWER, professor emerita, California State University at Northridge

VERN L. BULLOUGH, distinguished professor emeritus, University of Southern California

MATT CHERRY, executive director, Council for Secular Humanism

ALAN CRANSTON, former U.S. senator, California

DANIEL C. DENNETT, Center for Cognitive Studies, Tufts University

PAUL EDWARDS, editor-in-chief, *The Encyclopedia of Philosophy*

JAN LOEB EISLER, vice president, International Humanist and Ethical Union

ROY P. FAIRFIELD, Union College, Cincinnati

CHARLES W. FAULKNER, columnist, psychologist

THOMAS FLYNN, executive director, First Amendment Task Force

ADOLF GRÜNBAUM, Andrew Mellon professor of philosophy of science, University of Pittsburgh

PETER HARE, professor of philosophy, State University of New York at Buffalo

JAMES HAUGHT, editor, *Charleston Gazette*

HERBERT A. HAUPTMAN, Nobel laureate in chemistry

REID JOHNSON, dean, Center for Inquiry Institute

RICHARD KOSTELANETZ, author

PAUL KURTZ, professor emeritus of philosophy, State University of New York at Buffalo; president, International Academy of Humanism

GERALD A. LARUE, professor emeritus of biblical studies, University of Southern California

THELMA Z. LAVINE, Robinson professor, George Mason University

PAUL B. MACCREADY, engineer, founder/chairman, Aerovironment, Inc.

TIMOTHY J. MADIGAN, editor, University of Rochester Press

MICHAEL MARTIN, professor of philosophy, Boston University

JEAN C. MILLHOLLAND, executive director emerita, Council for Secular Humanism

MARIO MOLINA, Nobel laureate in chemistry

R. LESTER MONDALE, Unitarian minister emeritus

FERID MURAD, Nobel laureate, University of Texas Health Science Center–Houston

JOE NICKELL, senior research fellow, Center for Inquiry

ANTHONY B. PINN, associate professor of religious studies, coordinator, African-American studies, Macalester College

ROBERT M. PRICE, assistant professor of New Testament and biblical interpretations, Drew University

HOWARD B. RADEST, former head, Ethical Culture Schools

ARMEN A. SAGINIAN, executive director, New Horizons

DAVID SCHAFER, emeritus research physiologist, U.S. Veterans Administration

THEODORE SCHICK JR., professor of philosophy, Muhlenberg College

HERBERT SILVERMAN, professor of mathematics, College of Charleston

WARREN ALLEN SMITH, author

VICTOR J. STENGER, professor of physics, University of Hawaii at Manoa

ROBERT B. TAPP, professor of education, University of Minnesota; dean, Humanist Institute

JILL TARTER, Bernard M. Oliver Chair, SETI Institute

CAROL ANNE TAVRIS, social scientist, author

RICHARD TAYLOR, professor of philosophy, University of Rochester

YERVANT TERZIAN, David C. Duncan professor in the physical sciences, Cornell University

LIONEL TIGER, professor of anthropology, Rutgers–the State University of New Jersey

LEWIS VAUGHN, editor, *Free Inquiry*

IBN WARRAQ, author

EDWARD O. WILSON, Museum of Comparative Zoology, Harvard University

YUGOSLAVIA

JOVAN BABIC, chair, Faculty of Philosophy, University of Belgrade

DOBRICA ĆOSIĆ, author, former president, Federal Republic of Yugoslavia

SVETOZAR STOJANOVIĆ, professor and president, Institute of Philosophy, University of Belgrade